# Finding Jesus
# in the Psalms:
# Leader Guide

# Finding Jesus in the Psalms:
# A Lenten Journey

Finding Jesus in the Psalms
978-1-7910-2674-5
978-1-7910-2675-2 *eBook*

Finding Jesus in the Psalms: DVD
978-1-7910-2678-3

Finding Jesus in the Psalms: Leader Guide
978-1-7910-2676-9
978-1-7910-2677-6 *eBook*

# BARB ROOSE

# FINDING
# JESUS
## IN THE
# PSALMS

*A Lenten Journey*

## LEADER GUIDE

Abingdon Press | Nashville

Finding Jesus in the Psalms:
A Lenten Journey
Leader Guide

978-1-7910-2676-9

MANUFACTURED IN THE UNITED STATES OF AMERICA

# CONTENTS

# To the Leader

First things first: Thank you!

Thank you for your willingness to facilitate a group study of Barb Roose's *Finding Jesus in the Psalms*. You stand firm in an ancient and ongoing tradition of inviting disciples into the rich and essential exploration of God's word for God's people. It is hard to emphasize how important and valuable your leadership is. We live in a day and age where many people feel they are simply too busy and too overwhelmed to engage in biblical study and reflection. You are a gift to the group you will lead.

The modern-day Christian church in the United States is becoming disconnected from the poetry and lyricism of the Book of Psalms. In efforts to make the church more accessible and attractive to newcomers unfamiliar with traditional Christian ritual and practice, the recitation of the Psalter in worship has all but been eliminated. Once central to weekly Christian worship, the Psalms have been relegated to the fringes, and many newer Christians have little or no connection with these ancient works.

Even among longtime church goers and Bible students, the Psalms often do not receive the same attention of the Gospels, the letters of Paul, other early Christian church writings, or the Law and the Prophets of the Old Testament. You are providing a much needed opportunity for people to rediscover and recover the glorious inspiration of the Psalms.

Another aspect of our current reality is that, for the vast majority, church is an hour or so for worship, and not always on a weekly basis. Exploration together in small groups is an essential part of our spiritual formation, but one not taken advantage of by many Christian believers. This exploration of the Psalms offers participants an excellent resource that will make their worship and spiritual development that much more meaningful.

When Christians gather to study scripture, to discuss theological questions, and to seek meaning and understanding of God's will, the Holy Spirit is always present and active. The study of the Psalms is worshipful work. It is prayerful work. And it is immersion in the holy writings of a very different time, place, and culture.

## The Purpose of this Guide

Barb Roose has written a clear and concise study of a number of Psalms and other biblical writings that focus on revelation of Jesus the Christ. Seasoned study leaders will have no problem discovering a wealth of observations, questions, perspectives, and epiphanies from her fine writing, but we make no assumptions about those who volunteer to lead this exploration. Everything offered in this Leader Guide could have the words "suggested" or "optional" attached. What is contained in this guidebook are bits of information and trivia, questions for personal reflection and group discussion, exercises, and recommendations intended to supplement and complement the content of the book and the planning of the teacher.

In most cases, there will be more suggestions than can be used in any one session. As you become familiar with the character and chemistry of your particular group, you may find certain questions and recommendations that fit better. You are the ultimate authority deciding what will work best with your leading style and the needs and preferences of your group.

## Session Format

The suggested session outline will work well with a one-hour class but can easily be expanded to ninety minutes or longer. The proposed design seeks to cover the key points raised in the study materials, but also to engage the group in interactive discussion that allows all participants to share (as they feel comfortable).

## Getting Started

- Welcome – greet participants as they arrive; make nametags available if needed
- Invitation to Focus – Clearing the Clouds
- Take a few moments to invite people to name any burdens, concerns, distractions, or anxieties they may be carrying with them, and encourage them to offer them to God in this time so that they might be more fully focused in the study time together.
- Opening Prayer (provided for each session, or use your own)
- Summary of Objectives for the Session
- Summary of Key Points from the Study Materials

## Journeying Together

- Read the Psalms aloud (perhaps use two different translations or versions)
- Reflections on the Passage
  - ◊ *Context*—who is writing, who is the audience, what was happening at the time, what is being communicated?
  - ◊ *Connection*—what relationships, images, symbols, metaphors, or prophetic words does the scripture use to convey its meaning?
  - ◊ *Jesus-Glasses*—where does the passage directly or indirectly reference or allude to the Messiah, revealed in Jesus of Nazareth?
- Questions for Reflection and Discussion
- So What?
  - ◊ What impact is our study of the Psalms having on our thinking about and understanding of God, God's incarnation in Jesus Christ, and our call to faithful discipleship?

- Looking Ahead—Preview of the Upcoming Session
- Closing Prayer (provided for each session, or use your own)

# Helpful Hints

### Engaging with the Psalms

Perhaps you are very familiar with the literary form we call the Psalms, even having a few that you can recite in part or in whole from memory. However, if you are like most people, the Psalms are less well known and less studied than many other parts of the Bible. Barb Roose chose a specific handful of psalms that point directly to the life and ministry of Jesus, fulfilling the long-expected arrival of the Messiah. Yet, these psalms are select threads in a glorious tapestry of praise and lament, hope and despair, faith and doubt, joy and suffering.

As the leader of this study, it may prove invaluable to take time each day to read three to five psalms. Do this prayerfully, devotionally. Open your heart and mind to the indwelling of God's Holy Spirit. Don't just think the psalms but feel the psalms. Try to enter into the spirit and energy of the Psalms. There are few more emotionally charged writings in our Hebrew and Christian scriptures than these psalms.

If reading is a preferred means of learning for you, C. S. Lewis's *Reflections on the Psalms*, or Walter Brueggemann's *Praying the Psalms* may give you a broader base and perspective from which to facilitate the study. Barb Roose also recommends a number of YouTube videos in footnotes throughout the study materials. These provide excellent supplemental information from which to lead the discussion.

### Background of the Psalms

It can be helpful to remind your group that the Psalms were originally composed in Hebrew and underwent many modifications in a predominantly oral culture. The Psalms were intended to be sung, reflecting some of the earliest hymnody and spiritual music. As they were written down, translated, then retranslated, much of the lyricism and rhythm was lost, though every effort was made to capture the sense of poetry and beauty. Modern translations, like the New

Revised Standard Version (NRSV), the Common English Bible (CEB), New Living Translation (NLT), and New International Version (NIV), and especially paraphrases like The Message present the Psalms as prose, ignoring some of the more poetic conventions presented in the original Hebrew. While this facilitates simpler reading and easier understanding, it makes it more difficult to fully comprehend the Psalms as they originally existed. The King James Version (KJV) is no longer the widely read standard that it once was, but many of the Psalms contained in this translation come closest to retaining the beauty and melody intended.

Because the Psalms emerged from an oral tradition, they are best read aloud and heard by the gathered community. It is strongly recommended that you make time each week to read the assigned psalm(s) aloud, perhaps in multiple versions. One suggestion is to invite everyone to listen as the psalm is read, using first the lens of context. A second reading in another translation or paraphrase could be used for the lens of connection. A third reading, perhaps from the King James Version, could invite examination through the lens of Jesus-glasses. Invite different members of the group to read as they feel comfortable; not everyone enjoys reading aloud.

People also have different comfort levels with poetry, hymns, and sacred songs. It may be helpful as the group gets to know each other to talk about types of poetry, lyrics, music, and imagery that people find most valuable or least helpful. The Psalms are rich with imagery, metaphor, simile, and irony. It is helpful to remind people that the Psalms communicate on multiple levels, and that they are intended to reach the heart and spirit as well as the mind.

## Group Dynamics

Every group is unique, and there is never just one right way to lead a group. If you are leading a group that has been together for a while, where people know one another fairly well, and everyone is familiar with the patterns and practices that are most comfortable, you may be fine simply launching into the study beginning with the first week's material. However, if you are assembling a new group, or introducing new members into an existing group, you may find benefit from holding an orientation session. This will give group members an opportunity to meet and get to know one another, to set up hopes and expectations for the study process, to get an overview of the journey together, and to allow you as leader to get a feel for the overall group dynamics. This is an opportunity to "prepare the soil" for the seeds that will sprout, grow, and blossom over the course of the study. An Orientation Session outline is provided at the end of this chapter.

Some of the key elements of group dynamics for you to be aware of as you lead the group are simple but significant. Who are the talkers and who remain silent? Who reacts quickly and who takes time to reflect before speaking? Are people engaged? Relaxed? Are there side conversations? Do people seem to check out? It can sometimes be helpful to invite someone to assume the role of observer in your group, especially if it is newly forming. It can be difficult to both lead the process and monitor the members of the group at the same time. In new groups, it takes some time to develop trust and confidence, especially in situations where participants are asked to share personal thought and feelings. It can be valuable to have a second set of eyes watching the process as you deal with the content.

## Group Covenant–Ground Rules

One excellent way to lay a foundation for trust and healthy relationships is to create a group covenant that defines some shared ground rules and operating basics. Even if your group has been together a long time, creating a covenant can be incredibly helpful. Some questions to consider as you create a group covenant are:

1. What are some of the best group experiences you have ever had, and what made them that way?
2. What do you need in a group setting for it to be a good experience for you?
3. What kind of behaviors do damage to good group experiences? Are there things we can agree *not* to do, so that we make this a good experience for everyone?

4. What is one commitment you are willing to make to make this an excellent group experience?

Quite simply, a good covenant states what we will do to make our group experience positive, what we will avoid doing that makes it negative, and what are the basic expectations for our time together that we can all agree to. It is a good idea to print a copy with room at the bottom for every group member to sign their name, then make copies so that everyone has their own. This can greatly clarify expectations and makes accountability much easier.

## Suggestions to Help Prepare Yourself

- Pray for the leading of the Holy Spirit as you prepare for the study. Pray for discernment for yourself and for each member of the study group.
- Before each session, familiarize yourself with the content. Read again the book chapters and related psalms and other assigned Bible passages. Read additional psalms devotionally.
- Choose the session elements you will use during the group session, including the specific discussion questions you plan to cover. Be prepared, however, to adjust the session as group members interact and as questions arise. Prepare carefully but allow space for the Holy Spirit to move in and through the group members and through you as facilitator.

## Suggestions to Help Prepare for the Group

- Bring a supply of Bibles for those who forget to bring their own. Provide a variety of translations.
- Encourage participants to keep a notebook or journal throughout the study. Make paper and pens available for people who forget to bring them.
- Have nametags and markers available, especially if your group is newly formed and people do not know one another well.

- Decide in advance if you will provide any refreshments. Having water available is always a good idea. Some groups like to provide beverages; some enjoy snacks. In some cases, refreshments can be an unnecessary distraction, especially if individuals have allergies or dietary restrictions. You may want to determine with your group what forms of hospitality will make the experience most enjoyable.

## Suggestions to Help Prepare the Physical Space

- Prepare the space where the group will meet so that the space will enhance the learning process. Ideally, group members should be seated around a table or in a circle so that all can see one another. Movable chairs are best because the group will often form pairs or small groups for discussion.
- For most sessions you will want an easel with paper and markers, a marker board and markers, or some other means of posting group questions and responses.
- If you plan to use the recommended YouTube videos or other digital resources, you will want to set up and test appropriate equipment ahead of time.

## Suggestions to Help Prepare the Learning Environment

- Establish a welcoming space. Consider the room temperature, drafts, lighting, access to amenities, hospitality, outside noise, and privacy.
- Set up a small cross, candle, and/or other appropriate symbols to create a worshipful atmosphere.
- Create a climate of openness, encouraging group members to participate as they feel comfortable. Your attitude and energy will help set a tone for the group's engagement. The more comfortable you can feel in your role, the more comfortable the group will generally feel.

## Suggestions to Help Facilitate Each Session

- Begin and end on time.
- Honor the time schedule. If a session is running longer than expected, get consensus from the group before continuing beyond the agreed-upon ending time.
- When someone arrives late or *must* leave early, pause the session *briefly* to welcome them or say goodbye. Each change in the makeup of the group changes the dynamics of the discussion and should be briefly acknowledged.
- Involve as many group members as possible in various aspects of the group session, such as saying prayers or reading the psalms.
- Remind the group members at each session: honoring confidentiality is crucial to the success of this study. Group members should never pass along personal stories that have been shared in the group.
- Encourage participants to express their thoughts and feelings honestly but assure them that passing on a question is always acceptable.
- Give everyone a chance to talk. Some people will jump right in with answers and comments, while others need time to process what is being discussed. If you notice that some group members seem never to be able to enter the conversation, ask them if they have thoughts to share. If you notice someone dominating the conversation, gently suggest they hear what others have to share.
- Invite people to discuss questions together in pairs or groups of three. This allows everyone a better chance to share their thoughts and feelings. Pairs and triads help everyone stay engaged and involved.
- If no one answers at first during discussions, do not be afraid of silence. Help the group become comfortable with waiting. If no one responds, try reframing the language of the question. If no responses are forthcoming, venture an answer yourself and ask for comments.

- Encourage multiple answers or responses before moving on.
- Ask probing questions to help people delve more deeply. Ask, "Can you say more about that?" or "How have you come to think/feel that way?" or "What makes this significant for you?" to help continue a discussion and give it greater depth.
- Affirm others' responses with comments such as "Great" or "Thanks" or "Good insight"—especially if it's the first time someone has spoken during the group session.
- Monitor your own contributions. If you are doing most of the talking, back off so that you do not train the group to listen rather than speak up.
- Remember that you don't have to have all the answers. Your role is to keep the discussion moving and to encourage participation.

# Orientation Session Plan (optional)

## Welcome

Greet participants as they arrive; make nametags available if needed.

## Invitation to Focus—Clearing the Clouds

Take a few moments to invite people to name any burdens, concerns, distractions, or anxieties they may be carrying with them, and encourage them to offer them to God in this time so that they might be more fully focused in the study time together.

## Opening Prayer
## (provided for each session, or use your own)

*Loving God, we raise our voices today as millions have through the ages, offering our praise, crying out in need, sharing joy and despair, hope and fear, faith and anxiety. We present our prayers as psalms, poems, and songs that express our deepest emotions and desires. Hear our prayer, O Lord, and remind us constantly of your presence in our lives. We pray humbly in Jesus's holy name. Amen.*

# Summary of Objectives for the Session

- To get to know each other better
- To share hopes and expectations for our time together
- To preview the session outline for each meeting
- To discuss what will make this a productive and enjoyable experience for everyone involved
- To create a group covenant to set some helpful, mutually agreed upon ground rules
- To share within the group the participants knowledge of and experience with the Psalms, and with the Bible in general

# Summary of Key Points
# from the Study Materials

- Summarize the introduction of *Jesus in the Psalms* (pp. IX–XI).
  - ◊ To explore the Psalms for references to the Messiah and Savior we recognize as Jesus the Christ
  - ◊ To be mindful of tools of context, connection, and Jesus-Glasses (p. XI) that Barb Roose will employ throughout the study
  - ◊ To strengthen the understanding of the writings of the Old Testament as foundational for the understanding of the Christian writings that followed

# Questions for
# Reflection and Discussion

- Describe how familiar you are with the Hebrew scriptures contained in our Old Testament. What favorite books or passages do you have in the Old Testament and why are they significant?
- How do you understand the Old Testament to relate to the New Testament?

- What is your familiarity with the Psalms? Do you have favorite psalms? What are they and why are they meaningful to you?

## Looking Ahead—
## Preview of the Upcoming Session

- *Assignment for next week*: Chapter 1, Psalm 2, and Romans 8
- Encourage people to keep a notebook or journal throughout the study.
- Check to see if there are any questions.

## Closing Prayer
## (provided for each session, or use your own)

*Gracious and loving God, you know what fills our hearts and minds before we even turn to you in prayer. Be with us this week, guide us in our study and reflection, and bring us back together again, prepared to encounter your divine Spirit in our gathering. We give you our thanks and praise. Amen.*

# SESSION ONE
## Why Do We Need to Find Jesus in the Psalms?

Psalm 2, Romans 8

### Focus Scripture (for Reflection)

*So now there is no condemnation for those who belong to Christ Jesus. And because you belong to him, the power of the life-giving Spirit has freed you from the power of sin that leads to death. The law of Moses was unable to save us because of the weakness of our sinful nature. So God did what the law could not do. He sent his own Son in a body like the bodies we sinners have. And in that body God declared an end to sin's control over us by giving his Son as a sacrifice for our sins. He did this so that the just requirement of the law would be fully satisfied for us, who no longer follow our sinful nature but instead follow the Spirit. Those who are dominated by the sinful nature think about sinful things, but those who are controlled by the Holy Spirit think about things that please the Spirit. So letting your sinful nature control your mind leads to death. But letting the Spirit control your mind leads to life and peace. For the sinful nature is always hostile to God. It never did obey God's laws, and it never will. That's why those who are still under the control of their sinful nature can never please God.*

*(Romans 8:1-8)*

# Preparing for the Session

- Pray for the leading of the Holy Spirit as you prepare for the study. Pray for discernment for yourself and for each member of the study group.
- Read again the book chapters and related psalms and other assigned Bible passages. Additional suggested psalms to read devotionally are: 18, 45, 72, 93, 110, 132.
- Barb Roose references YouTube videos for this session. You may want to review these and decide if you want to use one or more in the group session.
  ◊ Stephen Burt's "Why People Need Poetry," https://www.youtube.com/watch?v=o8ZWROqoTZo
  ◊ Bible Project's "Overview: Psalms," https://www.youtube.com/watch?v=j9phNEaPrv8
  ◊ National Religious Broadcasters's, "H. B. Charles Preaches on Psalm 2 at NRB's Proclaim 19 Convention," https://www.youtube.com/watch?v=g0Y_QxFrfkg
- Choose the session elements you will use during the group session, including the specific discussion questions you plan to cover. Be prepared, however, to adjust the session as group members interact and as questions arise. Prepare carefully but allow space for the Holy Spirit to move in and through the group members and through you as facilitator.

# Getting Started

*Welcome*

Greet participants as they arrive; make nametags available if needed.

*Invitation to Focus—Clearing the Clouds*

Take a few moments to invite people to name any burdens, concerns, distractions, or anxieties they may be carrying with them, and encourage them to offer them to God in this time so that they might be more fully focused in the study time together.

## Opening Prayer (provided for each session, or use your own)

*Wonderful God, we gather to offer our minds, hearts, souls, and strength to you, asking you to inspire and encourage us, and grant us insights into your will for our lives. We rejoice in our relationship with you and with each other. Bless us, we pray, in Jesus's name. Amen.*

## Summary of Objectives for the Session

- To gain a deeper understanding of the Psalms and to see God's prophetic revelation about the Messiah to come in Jesus.
- To reflect on our own faith journey and to see how the Psalms speak to our shared human condition.
- To discover the sweeping scope of God's covenant from the ancient Hebrew culture through the time of Jesus up to our present day.
- To see God's guiding hand throughout history and to discern together God's will for the world.

## Summary of Key Points from the Study Materials

- Many different factors influence our faith development and understanding of God.
- We often read and experience the Bible in parts and pieces and are not always aware of the "big picture" trajectory, missing many of the ways that Jesus is the fulfillment of God's covenant promises throughout Hebrew history.
- Many of the things we struggle with today are things human beings have struggled with throughout the centuries and across cultures.
- No matter how great our understanding of God may be, there is always room for growth and greater awareness.
- If we do not consciously seek images and references to Jesus as we read the Old Testament, we will miss many important connections.
- We seek to broaden our understanding of freedom from the power to do whatever we want to the choice to discern and do the will of God.

- We acknowledge that true freedom and power belong to God, come to us from God, and are given that we might serve God faithfully.

# Journeying Together

Read Psalm 2 aloud (perhaps use two different translations or versions). Invite listeners to note words, phrases, images, or related thoughts they hear.

## Reflections on the Passage

- *Context*—who is writing, who is the audience, what was happening at the time, what is being communicated?
  - ◊ Attributed to King David. Biblical scholars will often use the term "attributed to David" because there is some disagreement about authorship in the Psalms. Different perspectives include:
    - » Actually written by David
    - » Written in David's name
    - » Written about David
    - » Written in honor of David
    - » Written by someone else entirely
  - ◊ Written in an age of warfare and power struggles, constant political and military intrigue, a difficult time for trust and security
  - ◊ A statement of faith that God laughs at human power struggles and that a day will come where God will bring an end to petty earthly violence, sending a Savior
- *Connection*—what relationships, images, symbols, metaphors, or prophetic words does the scripture use to convey its meaning?
  - ◊ Imagery of heaven and earth
  - ◊ Divine judgment as an "iron rod" to smash to pieces the worldly powers like "pottery"
  - ◊ Images of earthly kings bowing down and kissing the Lord and Savior's feet

- *Jesus-Glasses*—where does the passage directly or indirectly reference or allude to the Messiah, revealed in Jesus of Nazareth?
  - ◊ The psalmist uses the same language echoed in Mark 1:11 and Luke 3:22, "You are my dearly loved Son, and you bring me great joy." The parallels are direct and powerful.
  - ◊ Romans 8 provides a wonderful vision of what "the decree" of Psalm 2:7-9 will actually look like through Jesus the Christ.

## Questions for Reflection and Discussion (in pairs or threes)

- Psalm 2 sets a precedent for the structure of many Psalms. It begins laying out the folly of human activities on earth, followed by God's resolution for the future, ending with a call for response. How do you understand the promise of a Messiah to be a solution to our human folly and quest for power?
- The Psalms often speak to the things we humans struggle with. What are some of the things you struggle with? How does your relationship with God impact your struggles?
- What do Psalm 2 and Romans 8 tell you about God's will for our world?
- Barb Roose redefines *freedom* from the right of an individual to do whatever they want to "a life free from fear and fully alive in God's great adventure of joy and purpose for your life" (p. 18). How do you respond to this idea?
- Barb offers her Spiritual ABC's (spiritual attitude, behavior, character) (p. 22) and the rubric of green light (fully engaged), yellow light (cautiously, tentatively engaged), red light (resistant, disengaged). How do you rate yourselves of these three ABC's, keeping in mind her pastoral word to "be kind to yourself"?
  - ◊ *Spiritual Attitude*: What is your level of connection with God or willingness to live for eternal priorities?

◊ *Spiritual Behavior*: What do your normal actions or activities indicate about your level of obedience or surrender to God?

◊ *Spiritual Character*: How often do you present yourself to be Spirit-led, or when does your internal or external life look like Jesus?

## So What?

- What impact is our study of the Psalms having on our thinking about and understanding of God, God's incarnation in Jesus Christ, and our call to faithful discipleship?

## Looking Ahead—Preview of the Upcoming Session

- *Assignment for next week*—Chapter 2, Psalm 16
- Encourage people to keep a notebook or journal throughout the study.
- Check to see if there are any questions.

## Closing Prayer (provided for each session, or use your own)

*All-knowing and all-loving God, help us to see ourselves as you see us. Make us aware of the times we think we are in control, have all the power to run our lives, and think that this is freedom. Instead, free us to discern and do your will, so that we might understand real power and live a life free from fear and struggle. We praise you, O Lord. Amen.*

# SESSION TWO
## Finding Jesus with Us in Our Hard Places

Psalm 16

### Focus Scripture (for Reflection)

*Therefore, since we have been made right in God's sight by faith, we have peace with God because of what Jesus Christ our Lord has done for us. Because of our faith, Christ has brought us into this place of undeserved privilege where we now stand, and we confidently and joyfully look forward to sharing God's glory. We can rejoice, too, when we run into problems and trials, for we know that they help us develop endurance. And endurance develops strength of character, and character strengthens our confident hope of salvation. And this hope will not lead to disappointment. For we know how dearly God loves us, because he has given us the Holy Spirit to fill our hearts with his love.*

*(Romans 5:1-5)*

### Preparing for the Session

- Pray for the leading of the Holy Spirit as you prepare for the study. Pray for discernment for yourself and for each member of the study group.

- Read again chapter 2 and Psalm 16. Additional suggested psalms to read devotionally are: 11, 31, 62, 63, 91, 121, 131.
- Choose the session elements you will use during the group session, including the specific discussion questions you plan to cover. Be prepared, however, to adjust the session as group members interact and as questions arise. Prepare carefully but allow space for the Holy Spirit to move in and through the group members and through you as facilitator.

# Getting Started

*Welcome*

Greet participants as they arrive; make nametags available if needed.

*Invitation to Focus—Clearing the Clouds*

Take a few moments to invite people to name any burdens, concerns, distractions, or anxieties they may be carrying with them, and encourage them to offer them to God in this time so that they might be more fully focused in the study time together.

*Opening Prayer (provided for each session, or use your own)*

*O Lord, there are times when it is so easy to put our trust in you, but there are times when our trust is weak and we give in to doubt and anxiety, worry and regret. Walk with us through those times and be our strength when our own strength fails. We ask your guidance and support as we share in this time together. In Jesus's name we pray. Amen.*

*Summary of Objectives for the Session*

- To gain a larger perspective on the ups and downs of life and to reflect on the meaning of trust.
- To examine five lessons from David's life: belief in God's goodness, delighting in God's people, personal contentment, assurance of God's presence, and holding an eternal perspective.

- To think about death and God's promise of eternal life in the context of Psalm 16 and the promise of the "holy one" who is not left "among the dead" or allowed to "rot in the grave."
- To understand the connection Peter makes in his sermon in Acts 2, referencing Psalm 16:8-11 as a prophetic pronouncement about the resurrection of Jesus from the dead.

## Summary of Key Points from the Study Materials

- When we expect life to be fair, we will be frustrated; there are always times when life seems unfair.
- Life does not always make sense, and we can become disillusioned and distressed when it doesn't fit our expectations. Barb Roose talks about "If . . . then" thinking; if I do this, then this should happen. Too often, things don't work out the way we think they should.
- Psalm 16 is a powerful expression of trust and confidence in God.
- For God's people throughout their many challenges, defeats, and trials, songs of trust and the promise of protection gave them enormous encouragement and hope.
- The author of this psalm provides guidance to those who heard it about how they could live their lives faithfully and fearlessly.
- In many ways, Psalm 16 describes what Paul wrote to the church at Corinth, "for we live by believing and not by seeing" (2 Corinthians 5:7).
- As human beings, we have a very limited view of time, space, reality, life, and the future. Psalm 16 challenges us to expand our vision, to see things from God's vantage point.

# Journeying Together

Read Psalm 16 aloud (perhaps use two or more different translations or versions). Invite listeners to note words, phrases, images, or related thoughts they hear.

*Reflections on the Passage*

- *Context*—who is writing, who is the audience, what was happening at the time, what is being communicated?
  - ◊ Attributed to King David by Peter in Acts 2; modern scholars are divided over the authorship of this Psalm and many believe it was written in honor of David, thus perhaps explaining why it is identified as a "Miktam of David."
  - ◊ David is a fascinating character from scripture in that he was at times very powerful and at other times very vulnerable; at times very wise and at other times foolish; at times very certain and at other times very confused and unsure. He was faithful and fallen, saint and sinner, dishonest and redeemed. In so many ways David is an ideal human image, fraught by imperfections and yet always remade righteous by the grace of God. Through the highs and lows, God is David's constant companion and source of comfort and security. He never doubts that God is God.
  - ◊ While viewed by many as a man of great power, wealth, and prestige, David never lost sight of the fact that nothing of this world is as great as the simplest pleasure of God. David could have written Romans 8:38-39,

    *And I am convinced that nothing can ever separate us from God's love. Neither death nor life, neither angels nor demons, neither our fears for today nor our worries about tomorrow— not even the powers of hell can separate us from God's love. No power in the sky above or in the earth below—indeed, nothing in all creation will ever be able to separate us from the love of God that is revealed in Christ Jesus our Lord..*

- *Connection*—what relationships, images, symbols, metaphors, or prophetic words does the scripture use to convey its meaning?
  - ◊ The concept of "a refuge," (v. 1) a place of safety, protection, and rest, was powerful to the Hebrew people

who knew bondage, slavery, war, and persecution for much of their history. The fervent desire for safety and security is something many of us today take for granted.

◊ The image of "sacrifices of blood" (v. 4) was reprehensible to faithful Jewish believers, and the author's declaration that God is "my inheritance, my cup of blessing," provides a compelling irony when we consider the cup of the new covenant poured out in Jesus's blood at Communion.

◊ There is no concern about eternal life—it is not God's will that the faithful should remain among the dead or rot in the grave. We were not made for death, but for life, and the emphatic proof of that comes in the person of Jesus the Christ.

- *Jesus-Glasses*—where does the passage directly or indirectly reference or allude to the Messiah, revealed in Jesus of Nazareth?

◊ Both Peter and Paul reference the Psalm 16 in their preaching; Peter in Acts 2:25-28 and Paul in Acts 13:35. The passage was clearly understood to mean that God would not surrender Jesus to the grave, and that Jesus's resurrection fulfilled the prophetic promise. God's undisputed power over death was an important message of hope, especially to early Christians facing all kinds of persecution.

## Questions for Reflection and Discussion (in pairs or threes)

Barb Roose highlights five observations made by the Davidic author "how finding refuge in God blesses his life in the present as well as his future" (p. 31). The questions for reflection and discussion are based on these observations:

- *David believed in God's goodness.* How would you define goodness? How is God's goodness different from our human goodness? Barb draws a distinction between "God is good" and "God *is* good" (pp. 32–33). How do you understand this difference?

- *David delighted himself with godly people.* Think about the people you spend time with every day. What kind of people surround you? What makes them attractive to you? What kinds of people make you feel most comfortable and secure? What types make you less comfortable? Some people say that they do not need to be part of a church or Christian community in order to be a good Christian. What do we lose when we are not connected to a community of faith?

- *David was content.* We live in a culture in the United States that values accumulation, achievement, luxury, and prestige. What impact does the invitation to want more, have more, spend more, get more, and use more have on our contentment? We often talk about scarcity vs. abundance. What changes when we stop thinking about *abundance* and think instead about *sufficiency*? How do we differentiate *needs* from *wants*? Take some time wrestling with the question, "How much is enough?"

- *David was assured of God's constant presence.* How do you experience God's presence differently in good times and bad times? In times of crisis or times of joy? In triumph or defeat? Are there times when God feels closer or farther away? What makes the difference? Is it comforting, threatening, or both to think that God sees everything you do, knows everything you think, and that nothing can be hidden from God?

- *David has an eternal perspective.* We live in the here and now and we respond to what is right in front of us. It is easy to forget that at this very moment, billions of other people are having very different experiences from our own. What helps you keep things in a proper, non-anxious perspective? How do you best deal with worry, frustration, and anxiety? What helps you not become overwhelmed? What kinds of things cause you to feel bad about yourself and perhaps be too hard on yourself?

King David and Jesus both shouldered incredible responsibility and faced unbelievable challenges. Neither could have possibly managed without an invincible and massive faith. Rather than being swept away in the challenges as they happened, both held a "big picture" view, seeing the whole rather than the parts. The assurance of God's presence, goodness, and eternal promises helped both to surround themselves with like-minded believers who helped them stay content even when storms raged all around them.

## So What?

- What impact is our study of the Psalms having on our thinking about and understanding of God, God's incarnation in Jesus Christ, and our call to faithful discipleship?
- Of the five observations Barb Roose makes of David—God's goodness, surrounding himself with godly people, a deep contentment, assurance of God's presence, and holding an eternal view—which offer you the most grace, strength, and support in your own life of faith?

## Looking Ahead—Preview of the Upcoming Session

- *Assignment for next week*—Chapter 3; Psalm 23 and John 10:1-18
- Encourage people to keep a notebook or journal throughout the study.
- Check to see if there are any questions.

## Closing Prayer (provided for each session, or use your own)

*Loving Lord, even when we forget and are unaware, you are ever present with us. Help us to be mindful of you, to seek your goodness and closeness, when we are alone and when we are in community and open our hearts and minds to see as you see, that we might be content with today, and look forward with joy to tomorrow. We pray in Jesus's holy name. Amen.*

# SESSION THREE
## Finding Jesus as Our Shepherd

*Psalm 23, John 10:1-18*

### Focus Scripture (for Reflection)

A song for pilgrims ascending to Jerusalem.

*I look up to the mountains—*
*does my help come from there?*
*My help comes from the LORD,*
*who made heaven and earth!*

*He will not let you stumble;*
*the one who watches over you will not slumber.*
*Indeed, he who watches over Israel*
*never slumbers or sleeps.*

*The LORD himself watches over you!*
*The LORD stands beside you as your protective shade.*
*The sun will not harm you by day,*
*nor the moon at night.*

*The LORD keeps you from all harm*
*and watches over your life.*
*The LORD keeps watch over you as you come and go,*
*both now and forever.*

(Psalm 121)

# Preparing for the Session

- Pray for the leading of the Holy Spirit as you prepare for the study. Pray for discernment for yourself and for each member of the study group.
- Read again the book chapter, related Psalms, and other assigned Bible passages. Additional suggested Psalms to read devotionally are: 27, 54, 56, 125, 136, 150.
- Choose the session elements you will use during the group session, including the specific discussion questions you plan to cover. Be prepared, however, to adjust the session as group members interact and as questions arise. Prepare carefully but allow space for the Holy Spirit to move in and through the group members and through you as facilitator.

# Getting Started

## Welcome

Greet participants as they arrive; make nametags available if needed.

## Invitation to Focus—Clearing the Clouds

Take a few moments to invite people to name any burdens, concerns, distractions, or anxieties they may be carrying with them, and encourage them to offer them to God in this time so that they might be more fully focused in the study time together.

## Opening Prayer (provided for each session, or use your own)

*Patient God, we are thankful that you put up with us when we think we can do things better than you. We need to be reminded that you are our good shepherd and that we sheep are not in charge. Bless us, lead us, teach us, and love us we pray. Amen.*

## Summary of Objectives for the Session

- To explore the image and metaphor of the Lord as our good shepherd and to reflect on what that means for our lives today.

- To think about the power of metaphor and imagery to help us better understand our relationship with God and with each other.
- To share ideas about how our beliefs and understanding of God, heaven, eternity, and the Christian faith developed over time throughout our lives.

*Summary of Key Points from the Study Materials*

- God's Word meets us at different places and at different times in our lives and can offer very different meanings. It is important to revisit scriptures with an open mind and heart, ready to encounter new messages each time.
- The ancient and pastoral imagery of sheep and shepherds is a foreign and abstract concept to many modern readers. How has the importance and impact of this imagery changed over time?
- Barb Roose offers five important characteristics of the role of the good shepherd: Provider, Peacekeeper, Power, Protector, and Presence.
- A strong connecting bridge exists between Psalm 23 and Jesus's "I AM" passage in John chapter 10 placing himself in the role of the good shepherd.

# Journeying Together

Read Psalm 23 aloud (perhaps use two or three different translations or versions; highly recommend the King James Version). Invite listeners to note words, phrases, images, or related thoughts they hear.

*Reflections on the Passage*

- *Context*—who is writing, who is the audience, what was happening at the time, what is being communicated?
  - ◊ Widely considered a "psalm of David," a poignant and powerful reflection from one of the most powerful men in Hebrew history drawing on his boyhood role and identity as a shepherd.

◊ Written in a time of uncertainty and possible warfare, the language is one of trust, confidence, and the promise that God will deliver all.

◊ In ancient Israel, the reference to sheep and shepherd would have almost universal appeal and understanding. Sheep were among the most valued livestock, providing food, clothing, warmth, and trade.

- *Connection*—what relationships, images, symbols, metaphors, or prophetic words does the scripture use to convey its meaning?
  ◊ Agricultural and nature imagery—shepherd, sheep, green pastures, still waters
  ◊ Geographic imagery—dark valleys, paths and pastures
  ◊ Banquet and feasting imagery—provisions of food, drink, oil, and comfort in the house of the Lord

- *Jesus-Glasses*—where does the passage directly or indirectly reference or allude to the Messiah, revealed in Jesus of Nazareth?
  ◊ There could hardly be clearer connection than John 10:1-18 with Psalm 23. God as Lord and Creator is David's shepherd; God in the person of Jesus the Christ fulfills this role for all who confess him Lord.

## Questions for Reflection and Discussion (in pairs or threes)

- Psalm 23 is one of the most beloved, compelling, and widely known scriptures in the entire biblical canon. Why do you believe it has such meaning and power for so many people? What significance does it have for you personally?

- How meaningful is the metaphor and imagery of sheep and shepherd in your experience? Are their modern analogies that carry the same meaning but are more familiar? It has been noted that the gospel relationship of teacher/disciple is more applicable today: no matter how good a sheep you are, you will never become a shepherd, but if you are a good student (disciple), you may one day become a teacher!

- In what ways do you experience God as a provider? In many significant ways, sheep are vulnerable and helpless. What are some healthy ways to understand the statement "God will provide"? What are some less healthy and helpful ways to interpret this statement?

- Good shepherds are peacekeepers and offer safety and comfort. Most of us face multiple demands and challenges in our daily lives. What are some ways that God and your relationship with Jesus provide you with peace, calm, and comfort? What spiritual practices provide you with "green pastures" and "still waters"?

- What "restores your soul"? Barb Roose speaks of seasons of life, relationships, and choices we make that stir us up or calm us down. Where do you find true rest, restoration, and re-creation?

- How important is it to you to feel in control and in charge? What do you find most challenging to give over to God?

- It has been noted that doubt is not the opposite of faith, but that fear is the opposite of faith. Many of us avoid "the darkest valleys" and other places that feel unsafe, threatening, or dangerous, but one of the strongest promises and assurances of faith in God is a power that can overcome any fear and foster in us an insurmountable trust and confidence. Where do you experience God's protection and the light of Christ in dark valleys?

- Barb Roose repeats the sense of God's presence King David felt, and the importance of the shepherd's presence with the sheep. How do you experience God's presence in your life? What are some of the strongest images you have of God, heaven, faith, eternity, and the future that remind you of God's presence? Where did these images come from?

## So What?

- What impact is our study of the Psalms having on our thinking about and understanding of God, God's incarnation in Jesus Christ, and our call to faithful discipleship?
- At the halfway point in this study and our Lenten journey, how has your thinking about and understanding of the Psalms been affected? What new insights have you gained about the meaning and purpose of the Psalms?

## Looking Ahead—Preview of the Upcoming Session

- *Assignment for next week:* Chapter 4; Psalms 110 and 100, Hebrews 7
- Encourage people to continue keeping a notebook or journal throughout the study.
- Check to see if there are any questions.

## Closing Prayer (provided for each session, or use your own)

*It is not always easy to admit our weaknesses and to confess our deep need for protection, direction, and correction. We often feel that we can do everything better on our own. Forgive us for these moments of arrogance and selfishness and help us to accept the gifts of your love, grace, and guidance, Good Shepherd God. Amen.*

# SESSION FOUR
## Finding Jesus as Our Hope

Psalms 110 & 100, Hebrews 7

## Focus Scripture (for Reflection):

*He is the kind of high priest we need because he is holy and blameless, unstained by sin. He has been set apart from sinners and has been given the highest place of honor in heaven. Unlike those other high priests, he does not need to offer sacrifices every day. They did this for their own sins first and then for the sins of the people. But Jesus did this once for all when he offered himself as the sacrifice for the people's sins. The law appointed high priests who were limited by human weakness. But after the law was given, God appointed his Son with an oath, and his Son has been made the perfect High Priest forever.*

(Hebrews 7:26-28)

## Preparing for the Session

- Pray for the leading of the Holy Spirit as you prepare for the study. Pray for discernment for yourself and for each member of the study group.
- Read again the book chapter, related Psalms, and other assigned Bible passages. Additional suggested Psalms to read devotionally are: 2, 45, 72, 101, 114.

- Barb Roose references the YouTube video for this session: "Is Jesus God in Psalm 110:1 Debate" (endnote 10 on page 144). You may want to review this video and decide if you want to use it in the group session.
- Choose the session elements you will use during the group session, including the specific discussion questions you plan to cover. Be prepared, however, to adjust the session as group members interact and as questions arise. Prepare carefully but allow space for the Holy Spirit to move in and through the group members and through you as facilitator.

# Getting Started

*Welcome*

Greet participants as they arrive; make nametags available if needed.

*Invitation to Focus—Clearing the Clouds*

Take a few moments to invite people to name any burdens, concerns, distractions, or anxieties they may be carrying with them, and encourage them to offer them to God in this time so that they might be more fully focused in the study time together.

*Opening Prayer (provided for each session, or use your own)*

*Loving God, there are so many forces at work in our world to rob us of hope. We see so much pain and selfishness, violence and greed, aggression and disrespect. It is hard to keep our spirits up and our faith strong. Help us, we pray. By your Holy Spirit, allow us to see beyond the challenges of the moment, that we might hold fast to your promises for the future. We pray this in Jesus's name. Amen.*

*Summary of Objectives for the Session*

- To be reminded that there is often debate and disagreement about the meaning and intention of some of our scriptures, but that ultimately God's grace and understanding emerge from our questions, our discussions, and even our doubts and debates

- To engage more deeply on the relationship between David in the Old Testament and Jesus in the New Testament
- To gain an understanding of the evolution of our human understanding of God, illustrated by the way people translated and communicated names for God
- To share our thoughts and perspectives on judgment, justice, punishment, and retribution and how these concepts changed from the time of David to the time of Jesus, and even until today

## Summary of Key Points from the Study Materials

- Psalm 110 is framed as a conversation and a pronouncement. Barb Roose indicates that many scholars debate who is speaking to whom in this passage. Some believe that the conversation is between God and a human agent, while others believe that the Creator God of the Old Testament is speaking to the Messiah God to come in the form of Jesus. There are other interpretations as well, some simply believing that this is an ancient literary convention that underscores the magnitude and importance of the message to follow.
- Doubt, questioning, wrestling with information and perspectives is essential for a healthy, growing faith. Ultimately, each person must make up their own mind which interpretation is most compelling, meaningful, and relevant to their own context and situation. There are many critically important questions that cannot ever be fully resolved intellectually. This is why we are a people of *faith*.
- Barb Roose offers her perspective that Jesus is indeed the conversation partner in Psalm 110 and offers one more persuasive illustration of the Hebrew scripture's foretelling of Jesus as God's Messiah.

- This Psalm is a pronouncement of the ultimate victory of God over evil on the earth and all who live as enemies to God's will.

# Journeying Together

Read Psalm 110 aloud (perhaps use two or more different translations or versions). Invite listeners to note words, phrases, images, or related thoughts they hear.

## Reflections on the Passage

- *Context*—who is writing, who is the audience, what was happening at the time, what is being communicated?
  - ◊ Most scholars believe this is one of the oldest psalms of David, uniquely written in the third person. It reflects an ancient hymn form, similar in many ways to the parable/fable forms of the time of Jesus.
  - ◊ Written in a time of power struggles and some early fracturing within the tribes of Israel and Judah, it is a call to unity and solidarity in the face of foreign enemies and potential invaders.
  - ◊ It's a promise of ultimate victory if the people will stand united and faithful.
  - ◊ The introduction of the priest Melchizedek refers to a figure widely understood to personify holiness, purity, faithfulness, integrity, and justice. By reputation, no one could ever fault a priest "in the order of Melchizedek."
- *Connection*—what relationships, images, symbols, metaphors, or prophetic words does the scripture use to convey its meaning?
  - ◊ Imagery of making a footstool of the enemies. To our modern ears, a footstool might connote comfort and ease, a place to put our feet up and rest. In a hot, sandal-based, unwashed culture, feet were abominably unclean, and to place one's dirty feet on another person was the height

of insult and contempt. As Barb Roose notes, conquerors would place their foot on the neck of their victims. This was a vivid and shocking image in ancient Israel.

◊ Rulers and kings, competing powers representing the faithful of God and their enemies, are dealing with each other with violence and warfare.

- *Jesus-Glasses*—where does the passage directly or indirectly reference or allude to the Messiah, revealed in Jesus of Nazareth?

◊ Psalm 110 is one of the most quoted and referenced Messianic Psalms. It is an excellent example of "the now and the not yet" nature of many prophetic writings. The language indicates an immediate and current proclamation and pronouncement of what God will do. It also acts as a covenantal reminder that God's victory is an ultimate victory, and though the people of God may go through cycles of exile and oppression, each and every time God will prevail, and all enemies will be vanquished.

◊ Hebrews 7 makes explicit the connection between Jesus and Melchizedek. God establishes Jesus as the High Priest, "holy and blameless, unstained by sin. He has been set apart from sinners and has been given the highest place of honor in heaven" (Hebrews 7:26). Melchizedek was both a real person and an icon, someone who was both myth and reality (like an Abraham Lincoln or a Saint Francis of Assisi), whose stories and reputation made him larger than life. When people referred to Jesus as a priest resembling Melchizedek, everyone would have immediately been impressed.

◊ Psalm 100 is a victory hymn that answers the promise of Psalm 110. No matter what we may see with our eyes at the moment, God is the ultimate victor. The Good Shepherd God is also the conquering Lord whose goodness endures forever. Some in Jesus's own time were skeptical of his Messiahship because they were looking for the conquering king rather than the nurturing shepherd.

*Questions for Reflection and Discussion (in pairs or threes)*

- Who do you believe is having the conversation in Psalm 110? In what ways does it matter? Does the underlying meaning of God's ultimate victory change based on who is speaking to whom? Why or why not?
- Barb Roose raises a number of names translated in different times and places for God. *Elohim* is a term meaning "God" or "gods" signifying those who are divine. *Yahweh* was understood as the name of God and came to be viewed as too sacred to be spoken. (Literally, YHWH letters Yod, Heh, Waw, Heh, the vowels are uncertain). This name was Latinized to Jehovah (JeHoWaH). *Adonai* was understood as "my lord," generally indicating a human or divine being. When *Adonai* from Hebrew was translated into Greek, *Kyrios*, it was always capitalized and generally understood to refer to God the Father, or God the Son. Why do you think these distinctions were made? What difference do they make to you? Are there names or references to God that you prefer? Ones that make you uncomfortable?
- How do you understand the concept of "enemies of God"? Are unbelievers enemies? Are those who aren't Christian enemies? Do you see distinctions between non-believers and enemies of God? What are they?
- How do you understand the relationship between God's judgment and God's grace? What is the relationship between retribution and healing? How does Jesus as our hope move us from a desire for condemnation and punishment to reconciliation, mercy, and justice?
- Read Psalm 100 aloud (perhaps use two or more different translations or versions). What changes for you when you

can let go of the judgment and vengeance of Psalm 110 and enter fully into the joy and celebration of Psalm 100? How does this shift influence your understanding of finding Jesus as our hope?

## So What?

- What impact is our study of the Psalms having on our thinking about and understanding of God, God's incarnation in Jesus Christ, and our call to faithful discipleship?

## Looking Ahead—Preview of the Upcoming Session

- *Assignment for next week*: Chapter 5, Psalm 69, Matthew 26, John 18
- Encourage people to continue keeping a notebook or journal throughout the study.
- Check to see if there are any questions.

## Closing Prayer (provided for each session, or use your own)

*Lord God, you have given us hope by coming to earth as Jesus and abiding with us as Christ through your Holy Spirit. We are lost without you, and we too easily fall into doubt and despair. Lift us loving shepherd and bless us with your peace and assurance. Amen.*

# SESSION FIVE
## Finding Jesus as Our Strength

*Psalm 69, Matthew 26, John 18*

### Focus Scripture (for Reflection)

*I tell you the truth, everyone who acknowledges me publicly here on earth, the Son of Man will also acknowledge in the presence of God's angels. But anyone who denies me here on earth will be denied before God's angels. Anyone who speaks against the Son of Man can be forgiven, but anyone who blasphemes the Holy Spirit will not be forgiven. And when you are brought to trial in the synagogues and before rulers and authorities, don't worry about how to defend yourself or what to say, for the Holy Spirit will teach you at that time what needs to be said.*

*(Luke 12:8-12)*

### Preparing for the Session

- Pray for the leading of the Holy Spirit as you prepare for the study. Pray for discernment for yourself and for each member of the study group.
- Read again the book chapters and related Psalms and other assigned Bible passages. Additional suggested Psalms to read devotionally are: 4, 17, 41, 53, 88, 116, 142.

- Choose the session elements you will use during the group session, including the specific discussion questions you plan to cover. Be prepared, however, to adjust the session as group members interact and as questions arise. Prepare carefully but allow space for the Holy Spirit to move in and through the group members and through you as facilitator.

## Getting Started

*Welcome*

Greet participants as they arrive; make nametags available if needed.

*Invitation to Focus—Clearing the Clouds*

Take a few moments to invite people to name any burdens, concerns, distractions, or anxieties they may be carrying with them, and encourage them to offer them to God in this time so that they might be more fully focused in the study time together.

*Opening Prayer (provided for each session, or use your own)*

*There are times, O Lord, when life simply overwhelms us, when we feel all alone and without hope. We are sometimes misunderstood and unfairly treated. It is all too easy to sink into despair and self-pity. Forgive us and strengthen us, gracious God, that we might face all challenges faithfully, and trust in you that we will not be defeated. We humbly pray for your blessing. Amen.*

*Summary of Objectives for the Session*

- To understand the Psalms as prayers and petitions for strength in desperate and overwhelming times, available to us today, but used by David and Jesus in their own lives.
- To acknowledge that life is often unfair and that misunderstanding can cause great harm and suffering, but God's grace and comfort is greater than any human failing.

- To realize that God helps us face problems head on and not give into fear, avoidance, resistance, or defensiveness.
- To understand the importance of self-awareness and honesty in living God's will fully and well.

*Summary of Key Points from the Study Materials*
- Psalm 69 is a very human lament about being misunderstood, persecuted, mocked, insulted, and harmed.
- There are times when normal life becomes overwhelming, leading to periods of hopelessness and despair, even for people like King David and Jesus, but God is the ultimate truth.
- Everyone faces times where they feel misunderstood, unfairly or unjustly treated, and the Psalmist offers us healthy ways to respond.
- God gives us the strength to move through the difficult times, facing the challenges rather than running away from them or trying to ignore them.
- David is a model of integrity, merging qualities of humility, honesty, taking responsibility in a healthy self-awareness.
- Confession—a practice not fully appreciated in our modern culture—is a powerful means of dealing with the oppressive guilt, shame, and fear we often feel.
- Trusting God, seeing the good and the blessings in life and giving thanks, and holding fast to hope are decisions we make. We choose to have faith in God despite the challenges we face. Matthew 26 and John 18 mirror the commitment to trust God no matter what David displays in Psalm 69.

# Journeying Together

Read Psalm 69 aloud (perhaps use two or more different translations or versions). Invite listeners to note words, phrases, images, or related thoughts they hear.

*Reflections on the Passage*

- *Context*—who is writing, who is the audience, what was happening at the time, what is being communicated?
  - ◊ Attributed to King David, but some scholars note that the Psalm may refer to events that happened later in Hebrew history ("rebuild the towns of Judah," 69:35). Universally, this is referred to as "a Psalm of David," which could indicate either authorship or that it is written *about* David.
  - ◊ The demands upon monarchs are constant and many, and those in power faced opposition from within the kingdom as well as from outside. History indicates that David was a popular king, but the incredible responsibility and social challenges David faced meant that he must have encountered multiple periods of overwhelming criticism, contempt, and outright attack.
  - ◊ The sheer openly human lament and pain evident in this Psalm makes it relatable to so many people in so many situations across time and space. David speaks to the universal pain people feel when they are misunderstood, made fun of, insulted, and unfairly attacked.
- *Connection*—what relationships, images, symbols, metaphors, or prophetic words does the scripture use to convey its meaning?
  - ◊ Imagery of deep waters, floods, mire, and threat of drowning is prominent and reflects a total loss of control over what is happening.
  - ◊ Gossip, mockery, being made fun of for beliefs and practices, being unfairly treated result in hurt feelings and defensiveness. These are experiences people of all ages have in common.
  - ◊ Descriptions of justice, that those who act unjustly will have to pay for what they have done and said. This is a prayerful call for accountability and fair play.

- *Jesus-Glasses*—where does the passage directly or indirectly reference or allude to the Messiah, revealed in Jesus of Nazareth?
  - ◊ Jesus was often the object of scorn and derision. Luke 7:31-35 has Jesus addressing it directly:

    *"To what can I compare the people of this generation?" Jesus asked. "How can I describe them? They are like children playing a game in the public square. They complain to their friends,*

    > *'We played wedding songs,*
    > *and you didn't dance,*
    > *so we played funeral songs,*
    > *and you didn't weep.'*

    *For John the Baptist didn't spend his time eating bread or drinking wine, and you say, 'He's possessed by a demon.' The Son of Man, on the other hand, feasts and drinks, and you say, 'He's a glutton and a drunkard, a friend of tax collectors and other sinners!' But wisdom is shown to be right by the lives of those who follow it."*

    David notes the unfairness in Psalm 69; Jesus calls such behavior childish.
  - ◊ The passages from Matthew 26 and John 18 carry many distinct parallels, highlighting what Jesus contended with in his final hours before the crucifixion. Psalm 69 was referenced by Jesus himself in John 2:17 and 15:25. David and Jesus both lament their situations, wish for things to be different, but ultimately choose to trust in God, knowing that God's will is best.

## Questions for Reflection and Discussion (in pairs or threes)

- Barb Roose describes "Save me, O God" (69:1) as a model of "good and gritty prayers" that are short and honest. When have you experienced times where wordy prayers wouldn't come, and all you could say was, "save me, O God"?

- While we all deal with difficult challenges in our lives on a regular basis, what makes a challenge feel overwhelming, like "floodwaters are up to my neck. Deeper and deeper I sink into the mire; I can't find a foothold" (69:1-2)? How do you relate to the Psalm of David and the stories of Jesus in Matthew 26 and John 18?

- David and Jesus both cried out for help, asking God to do what they wanted, but both conditioned their appeals with the proclamation of trust—"I want your will to be done, not mine." What helps you to trust that God knows even better what you need than you know yourself?

- Share a time when you felt misunderstood, made fun of, or unfairly treated. How did this make you feel? How did you respond? How did you feel about the people who treated you this way? Psalm 69 does not talk about forgiveness, as much as it talks about retribution and justice. Jesus does call us to forgiveness (Luke 23:34) and offers an alternative to payback. What helps you move from a desire for reprisal to a place of forgiveness, from a hope that those who hurt you will be punished to a place where grace can be felt by all?

- When you are confronted by difficult and overwhelming situations, do you tend to meet the challenge head on, try to avoid dealing with it, hope it goes away, ignore it, or do you have some other way of dealing with it? Psalm 69 and the Matthew and John passages challenge us to deal with things head on, trusting that God will be with us. What gives you the assurance that God is present with you and that you do not have to deal with problems alone?

- The beauty and grace of Psalm 69 is that it honestly presents how awful it feels to be mocked, insulted, misunderstood, and unfairly treated. We have all been there! David and Jesus made the commitment to do God's will and be faithful to their responsibilities no matter how they were treated (though it still hurt them and made them feel bad). What gives you the strength and confidence to do the right thing no matter how you are treated?

- Barb Roose notes that David is admirable for his humility, his honesty, his acknowledgment of his own responsibility in what happens to him, and the integrity of his trust in God. She underscores the importance of self-awareness exemplified by both David and Jesus (though we know from David's story a number of times when his lack of self-awareness hurt him—and others—deeply). What helps you build a healthy self-awareness? Who do you turn to when you need help seeing yourself as others see you? How does your faith assist you in humility, honesty, taking responsibility, and growing in your trust of God?

- Barb Roose offers a very helpful invitation to confession and speaks of the restorative and redemptive power of confession. Her prayer exercise on p. 108 is a very good model. How does honest confession help us overcome guilt, shame, and fear in our lives? Group members may not feel comfortable sharing examples, but ask them to take some personal reflection time to ask, are there things in my life that I struggle with that I find hard even to admit to God?

- Barb Roose speaks to a growing suspicion and lack of credibility with modern organized religion. In many ways and places, the institutional church has failed to provide a faithful and holy witness in our world. Weak and flawed human beings have not always acted with honesty, integrity, faithfulness, and self-control. When one spiritual leader transgresses, it hurts us all. What steps can we take to restore the credibility of the Christian church and rebuild broken trust and respect?

- David and Jesus are both very responsive in their leadership, but they are not reactive. They are not stopped by obstacles along the way, thrown off course when things go wrong. Instead of giving in to hopelessness and despair, they make a conscious choice to trust God. They choose to look for the good, acknowledge the blessings, and give thanks. What most helps you to actively choose to be positive rather than reacting negatively? How can our communities of faith help us to look beyond the hurt and insult, the frustrations and the fears, to stay focused on the faith, hope, and love God provides?

- Have you ever been made fun of specifically for your faith or beliefs? Are there ways that you feel awkward or uncomfortable letting other people know you are a Christian? How others view us and think of us is important to us. But letting others dictate what we should think or say or do leads us to "sink into the mire" that David laments in Psalm 69:2. In Luke 12:12, Jesus promises that the Holy Spirit will be with us to guide us in knowing what to say and how to respond. What else could help us have more courage and confidence to share our faith, especially with those who do not know God through Jesus Christ?

## So What?

- What impact is our study of the Psalms having on our thinking about and understanding of God, God's incarnation in Jesus Christ, and our call to faithful discipleship?

## Looking Ahead—Preview of the Upcoming Session

- *Assignment for next week*: Chapter 6, Psalm 22, Matthew 27, John 20
- Encourage people to continue keeping a notebook or journal.
- Check to see if there are any questions.

## Closing Prayer (provided for each session, or use your own)

*Almighty God, we are so thankful that you are strong when we are weak, that you are calm when we are agitated, that you are love when we are petty, and that you are beside us every step of the way. Help us to see ourselves— and each other—as you see us, through the Jesus-Glasses of mercy, justice, compassion, and grace. Amen.*

# SESSION SIX
## Finding Jesus as Our Savior

Psalm 22, Matthew 27, John 20

### Focus Scripture (for Reflection):

*You must have the same attitude that Christ Jesus had.*

> *Though he was God,*
> *he did not think of equality with God*
> *as something to cling to.*
> *Instead, he gave up his divine privileges;*
> *he took the humble position of a slave*
> *and was born as a human being.*
> *When he appeared in human form,*
> *he humbled himself in obedience to God*
> *and died a criminal's death on a cross.*
>
> *Therefore, God elevated him to the place of highest honor*
> *and gave him the name above all other names,*
> *that at the name of Jesus every knee should bow,*
> *in heaven and on earth and under the earth,*
> *and every tongue declare that Jesus Christ is Lord,*
> *to the glory of God the Father.*

(Philippians 2:5-11)

# Preparing for the Session

- Pray for the leading of the Holy Spirit as you prepare for the study. Pray for discernment for yourself and for each member of the study group.

- Read again the book chapter, related Psalms, and other assigned Bible passages. Additional suggested Psalms to read devotionally: 5, 10, 38, 77, 109, 143. You may also want to read Isaiah 42:1-4, 49:1-6, 50:4-11, and 52:13–53:12. These passages are referenced here in the Jesus-Glasses section and offer support for the prophetic nature of Psalm 22 and the crucifixion of Jesus.

- Barb Roose references a YouTube video for this session: "Cross Culture—Psalm 22—Skip Heitzig" (footnote on page 145). You may want to review this video and decide if you want to use it in the group session.

- Choose the session elements you will use during the group session, including the specific discussion questions you plan to cover. Be prepared, however, to adjust the session as group members interact and as questions arise. Prepare carefully but allow space for the Holy Spirit to move in and through the group members and through you as facilitator.

# Getting Started

## Welcome

Greet participants as they arrive; make nametags available if needed.

## Invitation to Focus—Clearing the Clouds

Take a few moments to invite people to name any burdens, concerns, distractions, or anxieties they may be carrying with them, and encourage them to offer them to God in this time so that they might be more fully focused in the study time together.

*Opening Prayer (provided for each session, or use your own)*

*No matter how strong our faith, loving God, there are times when we give in to utter despair. We know better, but our hearts outweigh our minds, and our spirits suffer. From time to time, we feel abandoned, but we know deep down you will never leave or forsake us. Whisper the words of promise into our ears when we struggle, remind us you are with us. And help us to proclaim your goodness, mercy, and grace wherever we go. Amen.*

*Summary of Objectives for the Session*

- To see the clear and prophetic connection between the words of the Psalm and the life of Jesus the Christ.
- To offer a new way of thinking about scriptures and stories that have become too familiar and that we think we know completely.
- To encourage us to continue to question and seek and search in our faith journey, to better understand God's will and to comprehend God's vision for creation and our lives.
- To remind us that nothing in our earthly, day-to-day existence can separate us from the God who loves us and who sees completely that which we see and understand only in part.

*Summary of Key Points from the Study Materials*

- Some scriptures and stories can become so familiar to us, since we experience them year after year, season after season, that we may miss significant meaning and significance.
- Too often, Christians seek to rush to Easter and the Resurrection at the expense of fully engaging in and experiencing the pain and struggle of Holy Week.
- There are multiple ways to read and interpret scripture, and one important way we can enrich our encounter with the Bible is to move from a third-person to a first-person perspective; not merely to watch what happens, but to feel what happens.

- To better comprehend the power of the cross—once viewed only as a mechanism for torture and death, transformed through Jesus's sacrifice into an amazing symbol of hope and triumph.
- Seeking understanding—asking why—is an essential part of our human condition and our desire to live faithfully and trust God completely. Though God's thoughts are not our thoughts and we can never fully imagine what God knows (Isaiah 55:8).
- Memory—remembering who we are, whose we are, and all that God has done for us through history—is essential if we will stay faithful and don't give in to doubt, fear, and despair.
- No one is ever too far gone for God to save. God's grace and love transcends all human limitations; God will respond when we call.
- Offering God our praise should not be conditional on our feelings at the moment but should reflect our willingness and desire to always honor God. We do not simply praise because we feel good; we feel good because we praise.

## Journeying Together

Read Psalm 22 aloud (perhaps use two different translations or versions). Invite listeners to note words, phrases, images, or related thoughts they hear. You may also desire to read Matthew 27:32-54 and John 20:24-29 aloud. You may invite group members to employ Barb Roose's instruction to put yourself in Jesus's place.

Ask people to use all five of their senses as they listen to these passages:

- What do you see?
- What do you hear?
- What do you smell?
- What do you taste?
- What do you feel?

Pay attention to your breathing, your emotions, and the tension in your muscles. Make this as powerful a sensory experience as possible.

## Reflections on the Passage

- *Context*—who is writing, who is the audience, what was happening at the time, what is being communicated?
  - ◊ While this Psalm is identified as a Psalm of David, scholars have long debated its authorship and intention. We do not have a recorded story from David's life that reflects such deep despair and hopelessness. We know David and other royal leaders faced fierce opposition and challenge, but there is an abject and utter despair in the first half of Psalm 22 that raises questions. Some scholars believe that the images are a metaphor for all of Israel, and the suffering God's people have experienced under different oppressors.
  - ◊ There are few other Old Testament scriptures that are viewed as such clear and precise descriptions of the life and suffering of Jesus. The parallels with the Gospels and other New Testament writings are powerful.
  - ◊ Many of the Psalms share a simple, straightforward binary structure—the first portion is lament and petition, the latter portion is a proclamation of faith and thanksgiving. Psalm 22 is two Psalms in one; some of the most painful and desperate language and images followed by some of the strongest, most hopeful language in conclusion.
- *Connection*—what relationships, images, symbols, metaphors, or prophetic words does the scripture use to convey its meaning?
  - ◊ Imagery of physical and emotional pain, suffering, isolation and desolation, brokenness and humiliation.
  - ◊ Animal imagery, feeling lowly as a worm and seeing opponents as bulls, dogs, and lions intent on violence.

◊　A promise of jubilant proclamation and praise declaring God's goodness, greatness, power, and providence.
- *Jesus-Glasses*—where does the passage directly or indirectly reference or allude to the Messiah, revealed in Jesus of Nazareth?
  ◊　Along with the prophecies of the suffering servant in Isaiah (42:1-4, 49:1-6, 50:4-11, and 52:13–53:12), Psalm 22 offers validation for many of Jesus as the fulfillment of the Messianic promises of the Old Testament.
  ◊　Gospel writers, Paul, and other New Testament writers draw liberally from Psalm 22 and saw it as direct evidence and proof as Jesus as the anticipated Messiah.

## *Questions for Reflection and Discussion (in pairs or threes)*

- Barb Roose offers a very helpful suggestion to keep reading familiar scripture and stories fresh and new: shifting our perspective from the third-person to the first-person. How does Psalm 22 and the story of Jesus's arrest, trial, persecution, and crucifixion change for you when you enter the story yourself (pp.121–22)?
- Barb recommends the practice of "holding space"—of not rushing through the awful and painful aspects of Jesus's last days to get to the triumph of Easter. What changes for you when you intentionally spend time trying to experience the crucifixion in sensory terms?
- The cross of Jesus Christ is lifted up as a symbol of hope, emerging from a terrible and tragic event to become an emblem of hope, strength, and faith. What does the cross mean to you? What are some of the other symbols of the faith that hold special meaning and power for you?
- What are the significant "why" questions you carry with you? What aspects of our lives and the current reality in our world do you wish you understood better? If you had the opportunity to ask God just one "why" question, what would it be?

- Barb Roose raises this question on page 127 of the study: "Given an option between your personal agenda and God's plan, which one has the best chance of blessing you in the long run even if you've got to bear some painful crosses along the way?" What could help you be more accepting of God's plan and willing to let go of your own agenda?

- Paul reminds us in 1 Corinthians 13:12 that we humans see only in parts and pieces, but one day we will see the whole as God sees it. How does remembering the larger story of God's relationship with the Hebrew and Christian people help us deal with the challenges of today? What do we gain by being able to focus on the "big picture"?

- Have you ever wondered (or felt personally) if there are things so bad that even God can't forgive them? Do you believe there are people outside of the possibility of God's forgiveness and redemption? What kinds of things do you think God might not forgive?

- Barb Roose makes the point that our praise of God should not be conditional on our emotions; no matter how we feel, we should offer God our praise and thanksgiving. What makes this hard for you? Easy? In what ways does giving thanks and praise shift our attention from ourselves to God?

## So What?

- What impact is our study of the Psalms having on our thinking about and understanding of God, God's incarnation in Jesus Christ, and our call to faithful discipleship?

- What significance has this study had on your understanding of the Psalms?

- What has been most meaningful for you in this time together?

- What questions still remain?

- How will you use or share the experience you have had in the days to come?

- Take some time to express appreciation to the people who made this experience significant for you.

## Closing Prayer (provided for each session, or use your own)

*Eternal and immortal God, we see such a limited picture of your creation, your beauty, your power, and your truth. We too often give into our doubts and fears, lacking the vision to fully trust you and give our lives to you. Fill our hearts with the psalms, hymns, and songs of faith that will constantly remind us of who we are, whose we are, and why we are here. Amen.*

# Afterword

*Later that same day Jesus left the house and sat beside the lake. A large crowd soon gathered around him, so he got into a boat. Then he sat there and taught as the people stood on the shore. He told many stories in the form of parables, such as this one:*

*"Listen! A farmer went out to plant some seeds. As he scattered them across his field, some seeds fell on a footpath, and the birds came and ate them. Other seeds fell on shallow soil with underlying rock. The seeds sprouted quickly because the soil was shallow. But the plants soon wilted under the hot sun, and since they didn't have deep roots, they died. Other seeds fell among thorns that grew up and choked out the tender plants. Still other seeds fell on fertile soil, and they produced a crop that was thirty, sixty, and even a hundred times as much as had been planted! Anyone with ears to hear should listen and understand."...*

*"Now listen to the explanation of the parable about the farmer planting seeds: The seed that fell on the footpath represents those who hear the message about the Kingdom and don't understand it. Then the evil one comes and snatches away the seed that was planted in their hearts. The seed on the rocky soil represents those who hear the message and immediately receive it with joy. But since they don't have deep roots, they don't last long. They fall away as soon as they have problems or are persecuted for believing God's word. The seed that fell among the thorns represents those who hear God's word, but all too quickly the message is crowded out by the worries of this life and the lure of wealth, so no fruit is produced. The seed that fell on good soil represents those*

*who truly hear and understand God's word and produce a harvest of
thirty, sixty, or even a hundred times as much as had been planted!"*
*(Matthew 13:1-9, 18-23)*

Thank you so much for leading this Lenten study, *Finding Jesus in the Psalms*. Effective and transformative leadership is not about having all the answers or being the expert. Effective and transformative leadership is about being vulnerable, opening yourself to new experiences, trying new things, and trusting that whatever happens is meant to happen. You are a seed sower. Your job is not to make sure something grows. You don't have to pull the weeds. You don't have to spread the fertilizer. You don't have to water, and you don't control the sun. The parable in Matthew 13 should give you great hope and confidence: if only 25% of your seed finds fertile soil and takes root, you have done a fantastic job. The rest is up to God.

By leading this study, you helped people understand that the seeds of the gospel of Jesus Christ were sown throughout Hebrew history and the evidence is in our scriptures. By God's grace and goodness, those seeds sown in ancient Israel blossomed and flourished in the first century of the common era. Jesus is the fruit of God's fertile planting, and the Holy Spirit continues to produce fruit in and through us to this day. In many ways, the body of Christ of which we are all a part is a continuation of the fulfillment of God's incarnation today. And the fruit that God continues to produce through us is the "love, joy, peace, patience, kindness, goodness, faithfulness, gentleness, and self-control" that Paul speaks about in Galatians 5:22-23. We are the fruit yield that God multiplies a hundredfold, sixty-fold, and thirty-fold. As a study leader, you continue to sow the seed of the Word of God, you help make disciples of Jesus Christ, and through you God continues the amazing work of transforming our world.

God bless you!